I0811494

New York's Land and Natural Resources

Daniel R. Faust and Amelie von Zumbusch

PowerKiDS press
New York

Published in 2015 by The Rosen Publishing Group, Inc.
29 East 21st Street, New York, NY 10010

Copyright © 2015 by The Rosen Publishing Group, Inc.

All rights reserved. No part of this book may be reproduced in any form without permission in writing from the publisher, except by a reviewer.

Book Design: Chris Brand

Photo Credits: Cover, p. 7 Michael Melford/National Geographic/Getty Images; p. 5 Collection of the New-York Historical Society; p. 9 Superstock/Getty Images; p. 11 John Cancalosi/Oxford Scientific/Getty Images; p. 13 Marilyn Angel Wynn/ Native Stock/Getty Images; p. 15 Library of Congress Geography and Map Division, Washington DC; p. 17 Three Lions/Stringer/Hulton Archive/ Getty Images; p. 19 (inset) © Corbis; p. 19 Library of Congress Prints and Photographs Division, Washington, DC; p. 21 © Bettman/Corbis.

Library of Congress Cataloging-in-Publication Data

Faust, Daniel R.
New York's land and natural resources / by Daniel R. Faust and Amelie von Zumbusch.
p. cm. — (Spotlight on New York)
Includes index.
ISBN 978-1-4777-7331-4 (pbk.)
ISBN 978-1-4777-7284-3 (6-pack)
ISBN 978-1-4777-7330-7 (library binding)
1. New York (State)—Juvenile literature. 2. New York (State)—Geography—Juvenile literature. 3. Natural resources—New York (State)—Juvenile literature. I. Faust, Daniel R. II. Zumbusch, Amelie von. III. Title.
F119.3 F38 2015
974.7—d23

Manufactured in the United States of America

CPSIA Compliance Information: Batch #WS15RC: For further information contact Rosen Publishing, New York, New York at 1-800-237-9932.

Contents

A Beautiful State

From Niagara Falls to the Adirondack Mountains to the beaches of Long Island, New York State is full of natural wonders. New York is in the northeastern United States. It borders five other states, as well as Canada. The Great Lakes and St. Lawrence River form part of the state's northern **border**. In the southeast, Long Island stretches out into the Atlantic Ocean. The arm of the Atlantic Ocean that is north of Long Island is called Long Island Sound.

New York has many **natural resources**. Natural resources are things found in nature that people can make **goods** from or use for economic gain. Some of New York's natural resources are its rich **soil**, its 18.9 million **acres** of forests, and its many sources of fresh water. **Minerals**, including lead, talc, and salt, are also important resources.

Beginning with the Native Americans, New Yorkers have found many uses for the region's resources. The activities of the people living there have helped shape New York's landscape. They continue to do so today.

Thomas Cole made this painting of New York's Catskill Creek in 1845. Cole was part of the Hudson River School, a movement of mid-nineteenth century landscape painters who were inspired by the natural beauty around them.

Mountains and Valleys

New York is home to several mountain ranges. The Taconic Mountains are in eastern New York and western New England. They are part of the Appalachians, a mountain system that stretches from Canada to Alabama. The Catskills, west of the Hudson River in southeastern New York, are also part of the Appalachians. Though they are near the Appalachians, the Adirondacks, in northeastern New York, formed separately. The rock that makes up the Adirondacks is very old, dating back as far as 1.3 billion years.

Between 100,000 and 11,000 years ago, the **glaciers** of the Wisconsin Glaciation advanced and retreated over what is now New York, shaping the landscape. As they move, glaciers grind down and move around the rocks and soil below them. They carve out valleys and pull some of the chunks of rock they knock out of place along with them. Glaciers, and the force of the water that formed when they melted, helped carve out the Great Lakes, the Finger Lakes, the Hudson and Mohawk Valleys, and other places in the region. Most of Long Island was formed by glacial debris, the soil and rock that was left behind by glaciers as they melted.

Most of the Adirondacks are forested, like this area around Heart Lake. Unlike most mountain groups, the Adirondacks form a circular dome instead of a long range. Though the rocks that make the Adirondacks up are very old, they have been pushed to Earth's surface more recently.

Rivers, Lakes, and Gorges

There are many rivers in New York. The Hudson River is the state's longest. It starts in the Adirondack Mountains. The Mohawk River joins the Hudson near Albany, the state capital. The Hudson then flows south into New York Harbor, then into the Atlantic Ocean. The Genesee River flows north from Pennsylvania, passes through the city of Rochester, then flows into Lake Ontario. It passes through the Genesee **Gorge**, which is also known as the Grand Canyon of the East.

Lake Erie and Lake Ontario make up part of the border between New York and Canada. They are two of the five Great Lakes. Lake Champlain makes up much of the border between New York and Vermont. It is named after the French **explorer** Samuel de Champlain, who visited the lake in 1609. The Finger Lakes are located in the middle of the state. They are eleven long, thin lakes that resemble fingers. The movement of glaciers helped shape all of these lakes.

Lake Erie and Lake Ontario are connected by the Niagara River, one of the shortest rivers in the world. The Niagara River forms Niagara Falls when it spills over a cliff that is about 176 feet high. Niagara Falls is one of the world's largest waterfalls. This painting of the falls was done in 1831.

Leafy Forests and More

New York has cold winters and warm, sometimes hot, summers. The Adirondacks are the coldest part of the state. Long Island and New York City are the warmest. All of New York gets a fair amount of rain and some snow, with **precipitation** totals between 32 to 45 inches each year.

Many areas have rich soil that is good for farming. Today, more than 60 percent of the state's land is forested. Beeches, sugar maples, pines, oaks, birches, and other trees grow in these forests. Among the animals that live there are deer, beavers, black bears, raccoons, foxes, bobcats, and skunks. Hundreds of years ago, forests covered even more of New York.

The Hudson River **estuary** is another important New York **ecosystem**. Estuaries are places where freshwater rivers flow into the salty ocean, mixed by the tides. Estuaries have a rich mix of plant and animal life. Striped bass, blue crabs, and other sea creatures begin their lives there. The estuary's marshes are home to herons, eagles, and other birds. Huge numbers of oysters once lived there, but most are now gone.

The deer that are native to New York are white-tailed deer. These plant-eating animals are common in most parts of the state. New Yorkers hunted them in the past and continue to do so today.

Native Americans

People have lived in the area that is now New York for nearly 12,000 years. By 1500, several Native American peoples lived in the area. Some were Algonquian speaking, while others were Iroquoian speaking. Both groups traveled on the area's many **waterways** in canoes. They built strong houses to protect themselves from the cold, snowy winters.

The Native Americans built their homes, canoes, tools, and weapons from the wood, bark, and stones they found in the area. They hunted deer, wild turkeys, and other animals and fished in the rivers and lakes. They also made clothes and tools from the animals they hunted. The Native Americans grew beans, squashes, and corn. These **crops** all grew well in the **climate** and rich soil. Native Americans who lived along rivers, creeks, lakes, or near the ocean fished and gathered different kinds of shellfish. Indians living on Long Island also gathered quahogs and whelk from which they made **wampum**. Wampum beads were strung on cords or woven into belts and had many uses. In later years, wampum was even used as currency.

Both the Iroquois and Algonquians used saplings and tree bark to build their houses. Algonquian houses were called wigwams. The Iroquois lived in longhouses. This photograph shows a recreation of a dugout canoe and a wigwam.

European Settlers

In 1609, the English explorer Henry Hudson arrived in New York Harbor. He had been hired by Dutch merchants to search for a more direct water route to Asia. He sailed north from the harbor on the river that now bears his name. Hudson saw that the land had many natural resources, in particular beavers. Based on his reports, the Dutch set up **trading posts** in North America. The traders gave Native American hunters cloth, metal items, and weapons in exchange for furs, which were shipped to Europe to be sold. The trade in beaver fur was especially important. Beaver hats, coats, and gloves were fashionable, and, in time, the demand for American beaver furs led to a decrease in the New York region's beaver **population**, too.

In time, the Dutch realized that farming was more **profitable** than fur trading. New settlements were founded and the **colony** of New Netherland's population grew. Colonists cleared land for farming and built homes with local materials, like **sod**, logs, stones, and bark. In 1664, the Dutch surrendered New Netherland to the English. It was renamed New York after the English king's brother, James, Duke of York, to whom the king had granted the colony.

This map from 1639 may have been the work of the mapmaker Johannes Vingboons. It shows the Hudson River, called the Noort Rivier here, emptying into New York Harbor.

The Battle for New York's Resources

Even after they took over from the Dutch, the English were not the only colonial power in eastern North America. The French colony of New France **occupied** land in northern New York and Canada. England and France fought over the land and resources in this area. Most of the fighting was over the area's waterways. The Hudson and Mohawk Rivers connected areas to the north and west to the Atlantic Ocean.

In 1756, French, British, and Native American soldiers fought in the French and Indian War. The French and Indian War was part of a larger European war called the Seven Years' War. In 1763, the British won the war and took control of eastern North America. To pay for this war, the British imposed new taxes on their colonies. Many colonists were angry that they didn't have more say in how they were ruled. They had spent many years farming the land and setting up businesses. They didn't want to pay more money to Britain's king, George III. This led to the American Revolution, a war in which thirteen of England's North American colonies, including New York, won their freedom.

This illustration shows the Battle of Rogers' Rock, which took place near Lake George in New York in March 1758. Robert Rogers was a British officer during the French and Indian War. He led 180 soldiers on a mission to scout the area around Lake George, in hopes of learning more about the French soldiers and their Native American allies that were located there.

Waterways Help New York Develop

Like the rest of the newly formed United States, the state of New York grew quickly. New towns and cities were established, often near the state's many lakes and rivers. New York City and Albany had been built along the Hudson River. Rochester is a city that was settled on the Genesee River. The city of Buffalo was settled on Lake Erie, in western New York.

In New York State and around the country, **transportation** became very important. The Erie Canal was finished in 1825. This man-made waterway connected New York City and Buffalo and helped the state's **economy** grow.

The first **hydroelectric** generating station on the Niagara River was built in 1881. In 1896, electricity generated by hydroelectric stations along the river began flowing to Buffalo. The power it provided helped the city's **industries** develop. Today, New York State's large water supply is still used to generate electricity to power homes, **factories**, and farms. It also provides water for the state's large population to drink!

In 1901, Buffalo hosted the Pan-American Exposition to improve the relationship between North and South America. An exposition is a kind of large public fair. During the Pan-American Exposition, thousands of electric lights lit up the city. Here we see the grounds of the Pan-American Exposition and a poster advertising the exposition's Electric Tower.

PAN-AMERICAN
ELECTRIC TOWER 375 FEET HIGH
EXPOSITION: BUFFALO
May 1st to November 1st 1901

New York's Mineral Resources

New York's mineral supplies also played a role in its development. The Adirondack region has large supplies of lead, talc, and zinc. These are used in **manufacturing**. This area also has one of the country's largest supplies of garnet, a stone that forms in many colors and is used to make jewelry. Garnets can also be crushed and used to make sandpaper!

Stone, gravel, and sand found throughout the state are used in construction. Limestone mining has been an important part of New York's economy since colonial times. Limestone was ground up to be used as fertilizer. It was also used to make plaster and, later, cement. Clay and sand from the Hudson River valley were used to make bricks. New York State became a leader in the brick-making industry in the early 1900s. Natural gas can be found in western New York. Today, it provides energy to people throughout New York State and other nearby states.

The gas pipeline shown in this photograph from the early 1950s is owned by the New York State Natural Gas Corporation. Gas pipelines like this one bring gas to businesses and homes throughout New York State.

New York's Land and Resources Today

More than 19 million people live in New York State today. The state has changed a lot over the last century. In the early twentieth century, many people moved from farms in the countryside to cities. There are far fewer farms in New York now than there were 100 years ago! Starting in the mid-twentieth century, many New Yorkers moved from cities to the **suburbs** surrounding them.

Even though New York State has changed, farming and fishing continue to be important. There are almost 40,000 farms in New York State. They grow crops like apples, grapes, wheat, and cabbages. Dairy farmers across the state raise cows for their milk. **Commercial** fishermen make a living by selling the fish that they catch in Long Island Sound and the Atlantic Ocean.

Tourism is one of New York's most important industries today. People come from all over the world to see New York City and its famous skyline. They also visit the state's beautiful natural sights, such as the Adirondack Mountains, Lake Placid, Niagara Falls, and the Finger Lakes.

Glossary

acres: Units used to measure land.

border: A boundary line between two states, countries, or territories.

climate: The weather patterns of a place.

colony: A region settled by people from another land who keep their loyalty to their homeland.

commercial: Concerning or related to business or trade.

crops: The plant products of a farm.

economy: The way in which a country or a business oversees its supplies and power sources.

ecosystem: A community of living things and the surroundings in which they live.

estuary: An area where a river flows into the ocean.

explorer: A person who travels to a place that has not been known or studied before.

factories: Places where goods are manufactured.

glaciers: Large masses of ice that move down mountains or along valleys.

goods: Items which can be produced, bought, or sold.

gorge: A steep, narrow valley.

hydroelectric: Having electricity that is produced by flowing water.

industries: Businesses in which many people work and make money producing a product.

manufacturing: Producing goods.

minerals: Substances, such as salt or iron, that form naturally under the ground.

natural resources: The natural wealth of an area, including land, forests, water, and minerals.

occupied: Took up space in a place.

population: The total number of a specific type of living thing in a given area.

precipitation: Any moisture that falls from the sky. Rain and snow are precipitation.

profitable: Producing wealth or other gains.

sod: A layer of soil containing a mat of grass and grass roots.

soil: The top layer of Earth's surface in which plants grow.

suburbs: Small residential communities immediately outside of a city or town.

tourism: The business or industry of providing services to people visiting from another place.

trading posts: Places where people come to exchange goods.

transportation: The act of moving something from one location to another.

wampum: Beads made from clams and whelk shells that were strung on cords or woven into belts, and used by Indians in the Northeast as ornaments, in ceremonies, in diplomacy, or as currency.

waterways: Rivers, canals, streams, and so on that are big enough for boats to travel on.

Index

Primary Source List

Page 5. *Catskill Creek, NY, 1845.* Created by Thomas Cole. Oil on canvas. 1845. Now kept at the New-York Historical Society, The Robert L. Stuart Collection, New York, NY.

Page 15. *Manatvs gelegen op de Noot Riuier.* Created by Joan Vinckeboons. Pen-and-ink and watercolor. 1639. Now kept at the Library of Congress Geography and Map Division, Washington, DC.

Page 19. *Birdseye view of the Pan-American Exposition, Buffalo, May 1 to November 1, 1901.* Printed by Pan-American Exposition Co. Printed poster. 1900. Now kept at the Library of Congress Prints and Photographs Division, Washington, DC.

Page 19 (inset). *Pan-American Exposition: Buffalo.* Printed by Courier Lith. Co. Printed poster. 1900. Now kept at the Library of Congress Prints and Photographs Division, Washington, DC.

Websites

Due to the changing nature of Internet links, Rosen Publishing has developed an online list of websites related to the subjects of this book. This site is updated regularly. Please use this link to access the list: **http://www.rcbmlinks.com/nysh/nylr**